WAYNE L. GOOD ARCHITECT

TRADITION, ELEGANCE, REPOSE

First published in Australia in 2004 by

The Images Publishing Group Pty Ltd

ABN 89 059 734 431

6 Bastow Place, Mulgrave, Victoria, 3170, Australia

Telephone: +61 3 9561 5544 Facsimile: +61 3 9561 4860

Email: books@images.com.au

Website: www.imagespublishinggroup.com

Copyright © The Images Publishing Group Pty Ltd

The Images Publishing Group Reference Number: 356

National Library of Australia
Cataloguing-in-Publication data

Good Architecture: tradition, elegance, repose

ISBN 1 920744 04 5.

1. Good, Wayne L. 2. Architecture, Domestic – Maryland
I. Title. (Series: House Design. Series 2; vol. 2)

728.09752

Co-ordinating Editor: Sarah Noal
Designed by The Graphic Image Studio Pty Ltd, Mulgrave, Australia
Film by Mission Productions Limited
Printed by Everbest Printing Co. Ltd. in Hong Kong/China

IMAGES has included on its website a page for special notices
in relation to this and our other publications.
Please visit www.imagespublishinggroup.com

Dedication

"Guided by a natural inclination, I gave my self up in my most early years to the 'pursuit' of architecture." Eager to experience the workings of an architectural studio—rather than a road trip to South Beach, I set forth with a small portfolio of sketches and drawings of houses immediately upon graduating from high school. Twenty minutes into my first interview I landed my dream job and was put to work that same afternoon. I will always be grateful to the two principals of that firm, Tom Kamstra and Beck Dickerson, for taking me on and challenging me with the experiences and responsibilities that have guided me immeasurably in my pursuit of architectural excellence.

Over the years, it has become progressively perspicuous that my practice has tended to attract a certain clientele, which as a group exhibit a striking similarity of traits. Although broadly diverse in their individuality and sensibilities, each one shares in no small measure the distinct qualities of extraordinary intelligence, physical attractiveness, charm, wit, style, and taste. I could go on, but I'll only mention one more—a keen eye for fine architecture when they see it. Notwithstanding the aforementioned, yet another quality shared by all my clients, and perhaps most significant of all to successful residential design, is the leap of faith found in the generosity of trust and confidence each

one has placed in my office. It has been my sincere honor and pleasure to have worked with each one in creating architecture out of the profound diversity of circumstances and challenges that all of their projects have presented. In many ways, this book truly is for and about each one of them.

All architects rely upon the skills of the building contractors and craftsmen charged with realizing their vision in brick and mortar. I am indebted to the following for their fine craftsmanship and contributions in bringing out the best in my designs: Bert Winchester, Dennis Smith and Mark Orwig, Howard Freeman, Charlie Sleichter, Mike Adams, Robbie Tennyson, Joe Bohm and George Fritz, and Mark Wagner.

No architect works alone—and many individuals have contributed immeasurably to realizing my vision of architectural excellence. Limitations of space, but not gratitude, prevent me from acknowledging them each individually. The specific contributions of each one as well as those of many others are listed in the project credits at the end of this book. I extend my sincere gratitude to all those architects and designers who have worked with me over the years under the banner of GOOD Architecture.

A special thanks to my publishers Paul Latham and Alessina Brooks, and their staff at The Images Publishing Group for

their enthusiasm and encouragement, and for publishing this monograph.

After the initial pride and excitement of publishing a monograph comes panic over the monumental effort required to gather and organize nearly 18 years worth of project photographs, data, text, and other information. Many thanks to Laura Kaupp, a most talented and conscientious young architect in my office, whose tenacity of criticism, hard work, and drive, truly made it all happen.

I am grateful to Roger K. Lewis, FAIA, a most thoughtful and perceptive architect, professor, author, and journalist for taking time out of his busy schedule to prepare the introduction for this monograph.

I have always practiced architecture passionately according to the rules of a very simple philosophy taught to me by my third grade teacher—"if it is worth doing, it is worth doing well." I am most grateful to my wife Leslie for not bringing up the subject of our own unfinished house too often over the past 15 years while I have directed all my creative energy to assuring that my clients were first and foremost stylishly well housed.

Wayne L. Good, FAIA

Annapolis, Maryland
December 2003

Contents

Introduction

Architects entering practice in recent decades face increasingly numerous and difficult choices, some practical and others aesthetic. In what town, city or country to work? What type and size of firm to work for? Which colleagues, if any, to select as partners? Which clients and projects to pursue? How to balance the passions and demands of professional life with those outside of practice? And, of course, which philosophy of design to embrace and advocate in an era of countless, competing philosophies? These questions demand considering a daunting array of options, so daunting that the destiny of many architects, whatever their talents, often results not from deliberate, well considered choices, but rather from unexpected opportunities and plain old good or bad luck. Yet, once in a while, an architect comes along who determines his fate quite early because of deliberate choices and strongly felt motivations that subsequently are never doubted or questioned. Wayne L. Good is one of those rare architects.

Some who eventually become architects are in high school before even contemplating a career in architecture. Others discover architecture only after completing university studies and working in other fields. Growing up in Great Falls, Virginia, Wayne discovered architecture in the third grade after his teacher told him to "learn to trust your eyes" and "not to let intellect get in the way." Nine-year-old Wayne fell in love with design at an age when most kids, still discovering with wonder and fascination the real world's limitless phenomena, give little serious thought to how they will spend their adult lives. Indeed, professional aspirations at that age are mostly fantasy. Kids imagine themselves emulating the heroes they see in television shows, professional sports, video games and comic books. No fantasy for young Wayne. The books fascinating him were full of pictures and drawings of real houses, books about real architecture and real architects. That fascination with and love of books, like his passion for architecture, has

never wavered or diminished. A dedicated collector, his personal library contains over a thousand architectural titles, including a number of rare and valuable monographs. He is especially fond of books chronicling the work of early, little-known 20th-century American domestic architects, such as H.T. Lindeberg, David Adler, and Dwight James Baum; designers of traditionally styled country houses in America's cities and emerging suburbs.

Wayne always liked traditional, domestic architecture, and he knew early on that designing homes would be his calling. He recalls that in 1972 when he bought a rare copy of Lindeberg's 1929 monograph, at the onset of his formal architectural education, his colleagues scoffed. Who had ever heard of Harrie T. Lindeberg? And in 1972, when the diverse strands of modernism and its various dogma still held sway, why would any architect or architectural student be interested in traditional, domestic American architecture of the 1920s and 1930s? This was a time when European modern masters—Le Corbusier, Mies van der Rohe, Walter Gropius, Alvar Aalto, Eero Saarinen—continued influencing pedagogy and practice while younger American architects and educators—Charles Moore and Robert Venturi—were advocating a uniquely American, vernacular modernism. Most architectural schools taught students—and many still do—that design originality, inventive form-making, and personal self-expression are the highest design virtues, that every new building should make an unprecedented, perhaps even radical and revolutionary aesthetic statement.

Wayne Good thought otherwise and made up his mind early on, realizing that he would be the master of his own architectural education. He never bought into the prevailing orthodoxy of modernism, which when embraced by mediocre talents often results in woefully banal architecture. But in the late 1970s and early 1980s, he also recognized the superficiality of postmodernism and the effete, thinly crafted historicism that was its hallmark. Although clearly motivated by a profound admiration for a specific period in American domestic architecture, his aim is not revivalism or the creation of historical pastiche. Wayne asserts that the "evolutionary" development of the traditional American house along with the careers of its proponents, were irrationally marginalized in the early 20th century by the "revolutionary" forces of modernism. As a result, he maintains that

the place of the traditional house in American culture is today not widely appreciated. Thus, by illuminating this period of suppressed architectural history in his work, Wayne's goal is to inform his houses with a broader perspective on the past in order to inspire a culturally richer American house for the future.

A perusal of this monograph reveals another significant facet of Wayne's work—he is not wedded to any particular historic style. Consciously disregarding changing architectural trends and fashions, he believes that achieving enduring *style* is superior to faddish *styling*. Rather, he chooses to rigorously study the aesthetic qualities and technical characteristics of little known, high-quality, domestic architecture produced a half-century earlier, whatever its style, as a basis to create homes of today comparable in design, quality, and craftsmanship. Thus, a house designed by Wayne L. Good can be *contemporary* in its response to site and context, in its spatial organization and function, and in its use of construction products and systems, yet evoke a sense of timeless *tradition* in its form, façades, materials, and finishes. Most of his house designs are modern interpretations and reinterpretations of traditional ideas and compositional motifs, not replications of specific historic precedents or periods. Accordingly, you will not find a *signature* style in Wayne Good's work. His portfolio of custom-designed homes is as eclectic as the work of the many architects whose

monographs he has collected, read and analyzed. Every project derives its style specifically and uniquely from the nature of the site and the sensibilities of the client filtered through Wayne's artful eye.

In 1980, Wayne moved to Annapolis, Maryland, the state capital and, more importantly, an 18th-century town most of whose inhabitants are committed to preserving the city's colonial and post-colonial architectural heritage. He correctly believed that in Annapolis and the outlying Chesapeake Bay tidewater region he would find clients who would appreciate his sensibilities and talents, clients with the taste, the financial resources, and the motivation to build the kind of homes he wanted to design. He candidly acknowledges that he prefers working only with those who share his architectural philosophy and have the means to put it into practice. He often recites the architect's prayer: "May all of my clients with money have taste, and may all of my clients with taste have money."

With tongue-in-cheek, he describes his highly developed, early warning system that he calls "rat radar," always switched on when he initially interviews prospective clients as a means of screening those unenlightened or unable to work with him, to share his vision, or lacking the necessary financial depth to do so. But he is not a dictator or prima donna. Once a client retains him, he listens carefully and serves that client compassionately and diligently. This entails getting to know the client very well: learning what the client likes and dislikes; ascertaining the client's needs; deconstructing, critiquing, and reconstructing the client's program; wrestling with the client's budget, and often educating or re-educating the client about timeless aesthetic principles. He sees a client's house as a *portrait* of the client, not the architect, and its style as derivative of the client's stylistic preferences rather than a literal embodiment of those preferences.

Over more than two decades, Wayne Good has produced a body of residential work epitomized by environmentally sensitive siting strategies, robust but reposeful formal composition, richly tactile materials and thoughtfully resolved details. But many talented architects can make such claims, no matter which stylistic labels are applied. What makes Wayne's work exceptional— and reveals the breadth and depth of his design talent—is its qualitative consistency: the clarity and rationality of *partis* and expressive geometries; the elegance and harmony of interior and exterior details, and the successful evocation of the traditional but diverse architectural characteristics of the Chesapeake Bay region.

Inevitably, certain design biases or tactics pervade Wayne's work. Floor plans are always composed to create axial pathways, axially organized rooms and local symmetries. This is evident in the thoroughly modern plan of Dillow Hall, which is

nevertheless a veritable manor house whose materials and details recall the late medieval English architecture transplanted to the American colonies. Houses often consist of wings or pavilions linked together to avoid overly massive structures, to increase perimeter wall area providing more opportunities for natural light, views and cross-ventilation, and to embrace intimate exterior spaces. This strategy is exemplified by Asagao, a home inspired by 16th-century, Japanese Tea House architecture; by the Georgian inspired Love Residence organized around a motor court; by the modest, cottage-like Kyle Residence clad in forest-green, lapped horizontal siding; by the Tatum Residence, alluding to the language of log cabins at Scientists' Cliffs in Calvert County, Maryland, and by the stone, wood, and stucco House of Roggio influenced by English and American country house traditions.

Never to be seen on a Wayne Good house are flat roofs and vinyl siding. He prefers traditional, time-tested, natural materials— brick, stone, wood, stucco, plaster—and uses both invented details and, where appropriate, historically "authentic" details drawn from texts. Equally important, and crucial to maintaining high standards of craftsmanship, he insists that his clients include construction observation services in his contract, knowing that some contractors, with or without the client's knowledge, are all too willing to deviate from approved design drawings in the interest of saving time and money.

Wayne's professional colleagues have recognized his achievements. Often cited for design awards by Maryland and Virginia chapters of the American Institute of Architects, his projects have been published locally, regionally, and nationally in both the popular and professional press. Having created a body of residential architectural work of uniformly high quality and artistry, he was elected in 2002 to the College of Fellows of the American Institute of Architects, one of the highest honors bestowed by the Institute. This book itself further demonstrates why Wayne Good's name and work are justifiably celebrated. Given all this, what's next? Like many architects, Wayne hopes that all his future clients will be sufficiently enlightened and motivated to offer him the opportunity and challenge to design the kind of architecture he loves to design, and to provide the resources to do it. Perhaps he is about to encounter his most enlightened and motivated client yet, and also his most challenging. He and his wife, Leslie, live in a house in historic, downtown Annapolis, but Wayne plans to design and build a new home on 7 acres they own on St. George Island overlooking the tidal Potomac River near historic St. Mary's City, Maryland. It will be fascinating to see what he will create when he becomes his own client.

Roger K. Lewis, FAIA
Washington, D.C.

It's better to be good than to be original.

The course of American domestic architecture under the sway of modernism has been compared to that annoying moment known to mountain climbers—"when, after hours of toil in an unknown terrain they triumphantly reach the top—of the false summit." Early in the 20th century, avant-gardism became the predominant measure of quality in all the arts. European architects, artists, and intellectuals fleeing the wars immigrated to America with apocalyptic images of the brutality of the battlefield and the flu pandemic ruthlessly etched into their psyche. Seeking a new beginning, the artistic imperative became one of denying all association with the past. This propagated the notion that only perpetually new and original forms of expression could effect the artistic progress that would lead to a more optimistic future. Out of this dogma, originality arose as one of the most highly valued artistic qualities, along with the idea that it springs miraculously from the individual artist owing nothing to others or to the recent or distant past. Traditional architecture and art, which improves and advances through an 'evolutionary' process, over time, was summarily dismissed in favor of radical reinvention and the illusion of betterment through perpetual artistic 'revolution.'

American architecture, undergoing a kind of adolescent search for an independent identity, welcomed the new European dogma—ironically as a means of breaking free of the shackles of its formative European traditions. Without the same direct political experiences, motivations and convictions of the Europeans, American architects saw only the style and not the substance. William Van Allen, architect of the Chrysler Building in New York, voiced the emerging attitude when he proclaimed in 1925, "No old stuff for me! No more bestial copyings of arches, and colyums, and cornishes! Me, I'm new! Avanti!" It is this avant-garde obsession with avoiding even the appearance of repeating anything that might be recognized as having ever been done before, that has acted as a kind of architectural Sherpa guiding the American house on a rambling expedition, which continues to lead, with rare exception, to the limitless false summits of Mount Mediocrity.

Derided by proselytizing critics on the crusade of modernism and marginalized by generations of polemically blinded historians, a full and complete picture of the place of the traditional house in 20th-century American culture has been all but obscured. Consequently, the history of the American house remains in the 21st century, only half-told. While, most architects and students alike are very familiar with the iconoclastic architecture of Frank Lloyd Wright, Le Corbusier, and Frank Gehry, only a minority are aware of the existence of such early 20th-century master architects of the traditional American house as H.T. Lindeberg, Benno Janssen, David Adler, or Dwight James Baum, to name just a few. This selectively suppressed architectural memory unnecessarily narrows our cultural perspective while profoundly constraining the nature, character, and quality of what is taught, designed, and built today.

In 1450, the architect Leon Battista Alberti advised "Never let greed for glory impel you to embark rashly upon anything that is unusual or without precedent"—good advice for many things in life, but particularly poignant for those who create architecture. Today however, too many architects have their aesthetic 'cultural positioning systems' hastily programmed to navigate their careers into optimal position to be struck by the lightning of media celebrity ahead of the creation of good buildings. The mechanics of fame however, are such that most experience an artistic trajectory akin to Evel Knievel on a bad day—ignoring the reality that lasting architectural achievement is rarely the result of sensational leaps so much as measured

incremental improvement. While modernism cannot be held solely responsible for the plethora of design dreck we live with, it must accept paternity for the bizarre, complex, highly personal, and exclusive quest for architectural novelty that we broadly experience today as the cutting edge. Sitting quietly at the opposite end of the spectrum is the American nostalgic desire for a literal archeological re-creation of the past. Architecture must have room for new ideas and experimentation or it will stagnate, but without also informing our buildings with the memory of their cultural past, they are reduced to nothing more than idiosyncratic form.

In his 1927 preface to *The Work of Dwight James Baum*, Harvey Wiley Corbett writes, "in the home, all worth-while culture, taste, and artistic appreciation has its inception. Hence the domestic architect is in a way our most important artist. By his influence over the budding taste of youth, he helps

determine architectural excellence in other fields. If his vision is broad, his influence will be far-reaching." Yet formal study and design excellence in the American house remains a rarity. The ideal of realizing a uniquely American architecture has always been strong. Whether modern or traditional, the true course to a timeless and culturally elegant American house lies in a synthesis of both the past and the present.

Tradition, Elegance, Repose

Wayne L. Good, FAIA

1

Thompson Residence

From forest to farm to resort to summer haven to suburb, the Chesapeake tidewater region is home to a rich but disappearing architectural heritage of leisure architecture with diverse characteristics. The years after the Civil War brought rapid prosperity to America and the shores of Chesapeake Bay were dotted with Victorian amusement resorts reached by steamship and rail from Washington and Baltimore. The early years of the automobile saw the rise of romantic waterfront summer colonies such as Sherwood Forest with its green Adirondack-styled cottages, Scientists' Cliffs with its tradition of small chestnut log cabins, and Piney Point on the Potomac River with its graceful arc of sandy beach, Victorian gazebos, and screened sleeping porches.

This new summer and weekend house for a family of four was designed to recall the inherited architectural genetics of the region's casual summer camp traditions.

Sited on a very slender ridge surrounded by Valentine Creek and forested parkland near Annapolis, Maryland, this new house was designed as a series of hybrid, rustic, wood, stone, steel, and glass structures evoking the feeling of a rural camp.

One of the primary design features of this house is the tightly controlled choreography of arrival, entry, and the unfolding of both water and woodland views. From the auto arrival court, the entry sequence begins with passage through a narrow "dogtrot" between two small garages and then emerges onto a light-washed boardwalk overlooking a grass courtyard with a controlled glimpse of the water beyond. The entry foyer continues the choreography of water views within the house, while the main living room with its floor-to-ceiling steel windows reveals and frames the ultimate long water view and natural context of the creek.

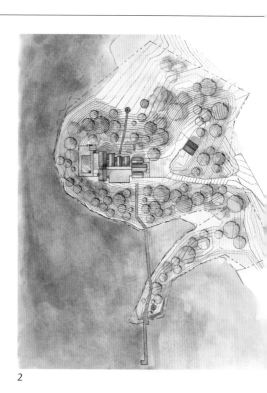

2

1   *East elevation standing on path to pier*
2   *Site plan*
Opposite *West elevation from base of chess tower*

4

5

7

8

13

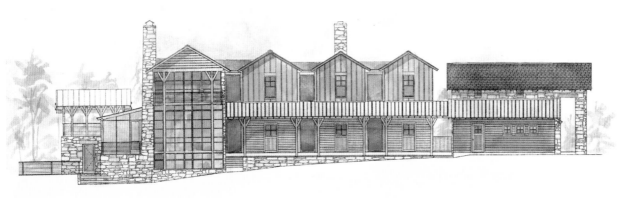

9

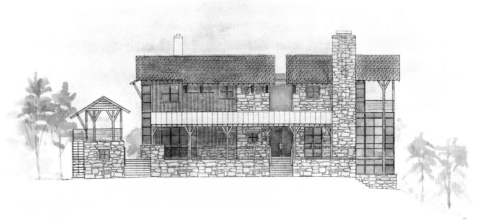

10

11

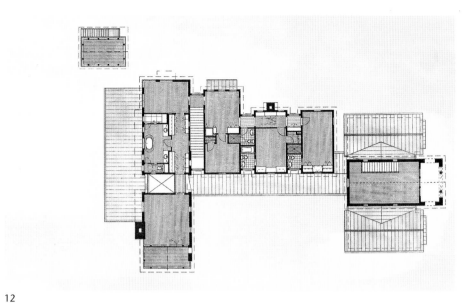

12

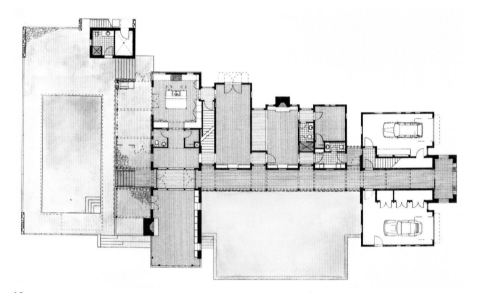

13

15

14

15

16

16 *River room*

17 *Master bathroom*

18 *Kitchen*

19 *Master balcony*

Photography: *Celia Pearson*

17

18

19

1 *Waterside view of new porch*
  addition at twilight
2 *Site plan*
Opposite *Upper-level deck of new porch*

1

Island House

This small 1930s waterman's cottage is located on Saint George Island, a low-lying, tidewater island, situated at the confluence of the Potomac River with the Saint Mary's River near Chesapeake Bay in Saint Mary's County, Maryland. Sited on the southwestern side of the island, this house had been compromised through a series of expeditious "improvements."

With spectacular westerly sunsets over the broad tidal Potomac River, the clients desired to replace a falling-down screened porch with a new, enclosed porch and roof deck that would capture the panoramic views. One of the primary goals was to design the new porch in such a way that it could be easily converted from an enclosed space to a screened porch or back at a moment's notice. Thus eliminating the ubiquitous "pain-in-the-ass" necessity of having to seasonally change and alternately store screen and glass panels.

Upon initial study, it was proposed that with marginal additional effort, the new porch offered an opportunity to substantially improve the overall aesthetics of the house while providing a unique architectural expression appropriate to the relaxed island environment. Although thoroughly contemporary in conception, the design expresses the vocabulary of the simple vertical board-and-batten buildings that recall the island's architectural past. The open framing of the upper porches was conceived of as "battens without boards" and continues the pattern of vertical battens in the framing and window muntins below.

To fully engage the panoramic views, the enclosed porch was designed as a convex wall of casement windows. When completely open, the French casement windows virtually disappear from the primary view angles inside the porch. The upper-level open porches overhang the south-facing glass

providing solar shading and allowing those windows to remain open and protected in a summer rain.

In addition to the porch, the project also included re-siding the house with vertical board and batten, the addition of a new entry stoop, a swimming pool, and a pool cabana. Although the pool cabana was designed in a much simpler mode as an outbuilding, its double gables reflect the new form of the main house. By similar design and axial relationships, the new additions serve to link the existing estranged buildings, creating a casual but cohesive compound of structures.

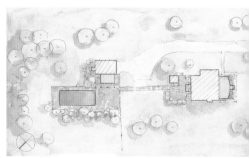

2

4

5

6

7

4 *Upper-level deck interior*

5 *New entry*

6 *Approach to entry*

7 *View of pool and pool cabana*

8 *Enclosed porch interior*

9 *Deck section/detail*

10 *Lower and upper floor plans*

Photography: *Celia Pearson*

8

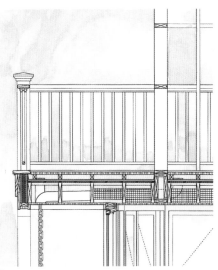

9

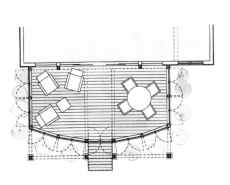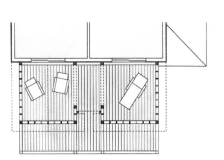

10

1 *View on approach*

Opposite *Entry pavilion facing garage*

Dillow Hall

In 17th-century Maryland, Saint Mary's City was home to one of the earliest expressions of architecture and baroque city planning in the new colonies. The country houses of Saint Mary's were either manor houses or plantation houses and were direct transplants from the English Middle Ages, reflecting the late medieval manner of building.

In 1694, when Governor Sir Francis Nicholson abandoned Saint Mary's City for Annapolis as the new seat of government, this rare and elegantly simple form of architecture was doomed to be lost. In Annapolis, the more current Americanized Georgian style was favored over the medieval which, by then, was considered to be "too English"—a first step in the American search for a truly independent architectural expression. Saint Mary's City was soon scavenged for its brick and other

building materials. Today, while all that remains of the old city are remnants of its foundations, scholarly archaeology is slowly revealing the unique character of this forgotten architecture.

Located in Saint Mary's County, Maryland, the site for this project is an extremely unique and beautiful peninsula bound by the Patuxent River to the east and Lewis Creek to the west. Virtually surrounded by water, the site is elevated about 30 feet above mean high tide and offers panoramic river views to Chesapeake Bay to the east, Solomon's Island to the north, and more contained and protected views of Lewis creek.

Thoroughly contemporary in function, the forms and details of this new house explore and express the unique vocabulary of its English roots found in the earliest medieval architecture of Saint Mary's City.

24

3

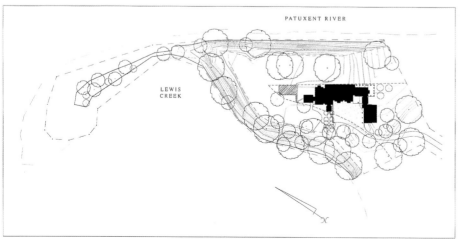

PATUXENT RIVER

LEWIS
CREEK

4

5

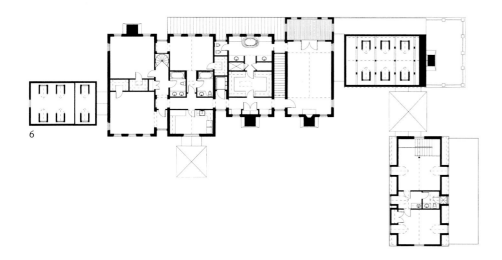

6

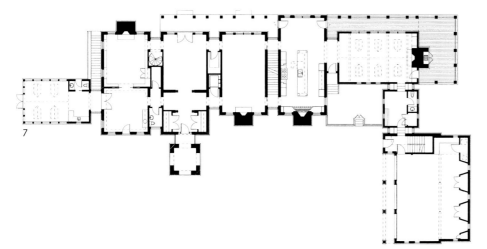

7

25

8

9

10

26

11

12

13

14

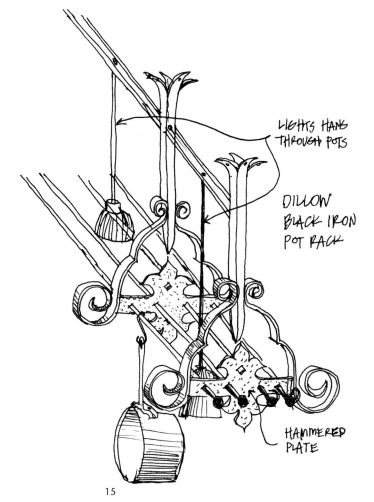

LIGHTS HANG
THROUGH POTS

DILLON
BLACK IRON
POT RACK

HAMMERED
PLATE

15

10 *East elevation*

11 *Library*

12 *West elevation*

13 *Kitchen with custom kitchen
island/work table*

14 *Garden room with custom potting
and cutting sink cabinet*

15 *Sketch of wrought iron pot rack*

Photography: *Celia Pearson*

Timberlane Farm

In the early part of the 20th century through the 1930s, America underwent a building boom in domestic architecture the likes of which has not been seen since. This was the era of the American country house and defined domestic architecture in the United States.

Built in 1937, Timberlane Farm is an exceptionally fine example of Georgian Revival architecture of the period. Composed in a classic Georgian block with dependencies, the five-part plan is elegantly proportioned and detailed inside and out. Notable architectural features include the gauged brick entry pediment with its surrounding detail, and the limestone waterfront porch, which was likely inspired by the design of Mount Airy in Virginia (circa 1758).

Though Timberlane's historic background is sketchy, original construction drawings indicate that the house was designed by the Philadelphia architectural firm of George,

Edwin, Pope, Albert, Kruse and built for one Hollyday S. Meeds Jr. also out of Philadelphia. It is believed that the house was originally built to function as a hunting and shooting retreat. Constructed entirely out of masonry, steel, and concrete, rumor has it that as a child, Mr Meeds experienced a family house fire and insisted that no combustible materials be used in the construction.

The project involved extensive overall interior and exterior remodeling and renovation of the main house, including custom design of cabinetry, paneling, furniture, and accessory items such as the kitchen dresser and wrought iron pot rack. Three small, outdated spaces functioning as a galley kitchen, pantry, and servant's room were combined to create a new kitchen/family living area. Two glass conservatories added in the 1970s were remodeled to serve as a breakfast room and an office, with new architecturally appropriate interior woodwork and finishes.

Large unfinished and inaccessible attic spaces were converted into two guest suites with a new private stair. New "his and her" master bathrooms and closets were created from existing, obsolete storage spaces.

Outside, a new swimming pool and pool pavilion complex, evocative of the original Georgian Revival architecture, were added. All mechanical and bath facilities here were placed beneath the pavilion to allow for 360-degree openness and exposure to light, air, and views. The pavilion is positioned flush with the coping of the pool, allowing access into the water via steps directly out of the pavilion. Overall, great care was taken to assure that the design of all new work was seamless with and respectful of the architecture of the house.

1   *View of main house and pool pavilion from north lawn*

Opposite   *Pool pavilion from pool terrace*

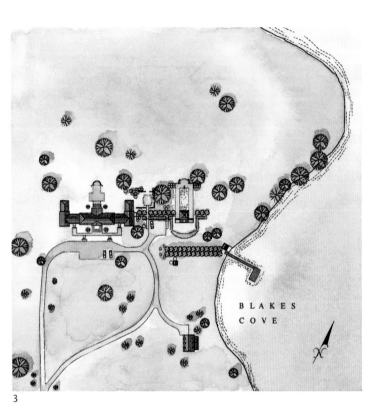

3

4

5

6

7

8

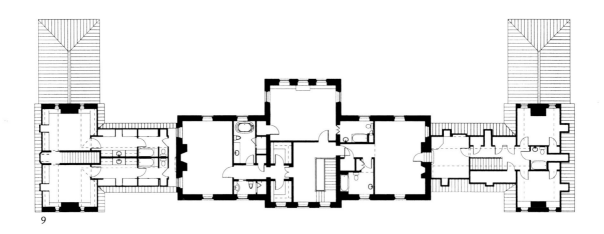

9

32

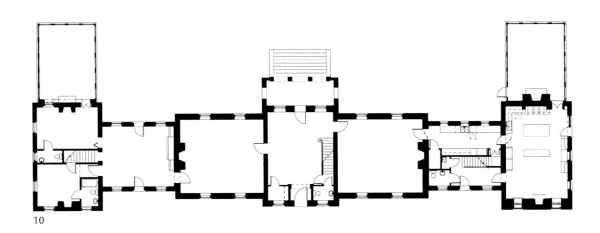

10

11

12

13

33

14

15

16

18

17

35

19

20

21

22

23

24

Photography: Celia Pearson (1, 2, 5, 6, 11, 20, 21, 22); Eric Kvalsvik (4, 13–19, 23, 24)

1

2

3

Moore Residence

Located in the heart of the Annapolis Historic District, this house is a circa 1885 three-story brick Italianate townhouse. Viewed from the street, the left-side two-story section was a later addition completed probably between 1925 and 1930 and detailed to closely resemble the original. The newly restored street façade presents original detailing and is a fine representation of the style and period.

Generally, the project program required an extensive combination of interior and exterior restoration, renovation, remodeling, and additions. Specifically, the owners wished to add a conservatory breakfast room with views of the garden; a mud-entry-room with new access to the basement; an updated kitchen; new bathrooms, and renovated gardens. The existing interior had been modified over the years to resemble a dark, anonymous boarding house and required opening up for better spatial flow and natural light.

The design approach to the new exterior additions was to create a strong genetic relationship to the Victorian architecture of the house. The rear and sides of the existing house were architecturally utilitarian with a simple two-story kitchen wing extending from the 19th-century portion and bisecting the rear yard. This condition was exploited as a device to segregate the formal side yard gardens from the utilitarian garage and parking area. This concept was architecturally reinforced in the expression of the two additions.

The conservatory was designed as a more flamboyant Victorian garden pavilion with the upper octagonal roof completely detached from the house. Sitting almost entirely in the garden and composed of mostly glass, this room contributes the most open and light-filled space to the house. The mudroom addition is architecturally downplayed and reflects the more straightforward, boxy and utilitarian parapeted roof forms of the

house in deference to the more whimsical garage, which was designed as an arrival focal point. Overall, the completed project represents an adaptation of historic architecture, acknowledging its roots while accommodating the aesthetic and functional expectations of contemporary lifestyles.

1 *South elevation*

2 *Approach view of garage*

3 *Conservatory entrance from garden*

Opposite *Street elevation*

6

7

8

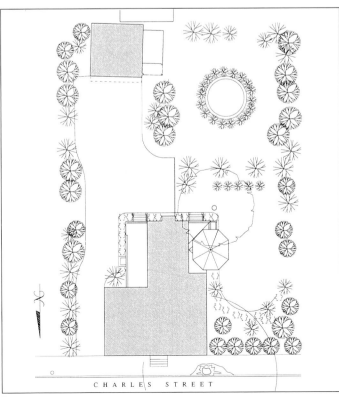

9

Opposite   *Conservatory from garden*

   6   *Sketch of garage*

   7   *Detail of mudroom/porch*

   8   *View of garage from garden*

   9   *Site plan*

CHARLES STREET

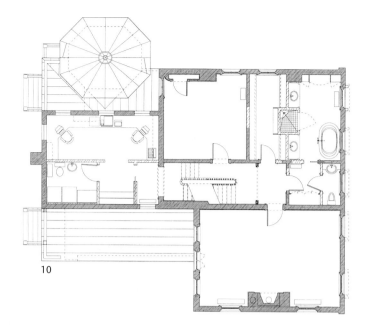

10

11

42

12

13

14

15

16

17

45

19

18 *Kitchen*

19 *Sketch of master bathroom*

20 *Master bedroom*

Photography: *Celia Pearson*

20

SITE PLAN
SCALE: 1"=45'
ACACIA ROAD

1

1 *Site plan*
Opposite *Entry pavilion*

Tatum Residence

In 1935, G. Flippo Gravatt and his wife, both forest pathologists in the Department of Agriculture, purchased 238 wooded acres on a high cliff overlooking the Chesapeake Bay in Calvert County, Maryland. This site was used to establish a summer colony of scientists and was named Scientists' Cliffs. An association of home site owners was formed and incorporated. The original bylaws adopted limited membership to scientists only, but were later broadened to include all college graduates or professionals. Today there are 200 home sites, a community house, tennis courts, swimming pool, maintenance office, dedicated parkland, and community vegetable gardens.

The architecture of Scientists' Cliffs developed as tiny (600-square-foot) iconic log cabins, many of which were originally constructed of solid chestnut logs weathered to a beautiful reddish brown. Over the years, Scientists' Cliffs has evolved into a full-time community

for the majority of its residents. Today, only a few of the early cabins remain intact with their original chestnut logs—most have been altered and enlarged insensitively. Although the community maintains written design guidelines and a design review process, later development within the community has tended to be architecturally arbitrary, out of scale and character, and of mediocre or poor design quality.

The client's program called for a retirement home of about 3500 square feet of living spaces with one-floor living on the main level, and guest accommodation, a family crafts room, and an office on the lower level. The new house was designed as a series of four small connected cabins, each about the size of an original Scientists' Cliffs cabin. Clad in a combination of log slab and vertical board-and-batten siding, our project attempts to demonstrate that current living patterns, and the desire for significantly

larger houses that come with full-time residency, can be accommodated within architectural forms that are compatible in scale, proportion, massing, and materials that appropriately reinforce the history of the original idea of Scientists' Cliffs.

3

4

3 *Exterior elevations*

4 *View from road at twilight*

5 *View from woods*

6

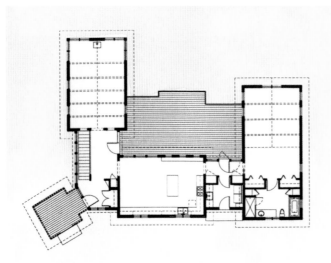

7

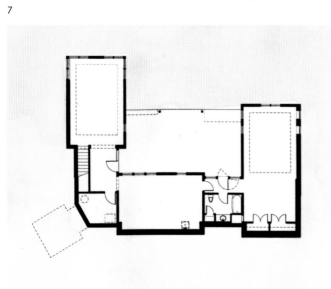

8

9

6   View on approach to entry

7   First floor plan

8   Basement floor plan

9   Entry hall looking into living room beyond

10   Kitchen

11   Living room

Photography: Celia Pearson

10

11

1

Mosquito Bight

Built in 1920, this tiny waterman's cottage is perched on a northern point of Saint George Island, a low-lying, tidewater island situated at the confluence of the Saint Mary's River with the Potomac River near Chesapeake Bay in Saint Mary's County, Maryland. At the beginning of the American Revolution, 72 British ships anchored off the 3-mile-long island and used the location to launch attacks on neighboring plantations around Saint Mary's City. In 1812, the British returned and sacked the entire place. Until 1851, the island was largely uninhabited and used primarily for grazing livestock. Subsequently, parcels of land were sold off including Ball's Point, the site of this project. Until the mid-20th century, the island was inhabited by working watermen and their families with names that are derivations of those found on the register of the Ark and the Dove. Today, the island is home to a mix of "old timers" and a growing population of weekend "money-people."

One of only a handful of unaltered early-20th-century vernacular cottages remaining on the island, the original prior owners made their living off the local waters—a way of life, which although governed by frugality and practicality, managed to express a degree of architectural delight in their home's nearly iconic image of domesticity. Probably built with the help of friends and relatives, the 675-square-foot floor plan is a basic four-room cottage and makes every square inch count with a unique configuration of no formal entry—the two front rooms (living room and bed room) each have doors directly onto the front porch. Another side door enters directly into the kitchen. Originally built without plumbing or electricity, the old privy and hand water pump still remain. Judging from nearly identical cabinetry in later neighboring houses, the carpenter-built cottage kitchen cabinets were likely added sometime in the mid 1930s.

Given the charming, nostalgic and pure architectural imagery of the place, it was decided that restraint should govern the design process in order to assure that the patina of time was not lost. The goal of the project was therefore to "respect, restore, and revive" while avoiding the appearance that "an architect had hit it." Indeed, the most prominent "new" design contribution to the cottage was in re-screening the front porch and the addition of a new decorative screened door simply reflecting the small diamond window in the attic gable. Out back, a severely dilapidated 12-foot by 18-foot boatshed was renovated and adaptively converted into a guest "bunkie" maintaining as much original material as possible. A vernacular raised-bed herb, vegetable, and flower garden was added as an organizing element to the outbuildings. All work was done in a manner that avoided artificial perfection, while enhancing the casual unpretentious atmosphere of a weekend fishing retreat.

2

3

4

6

7

54

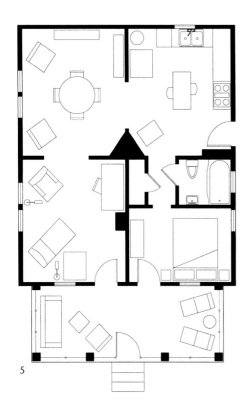

5

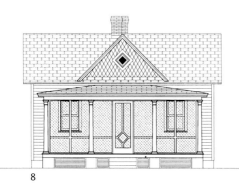

8

9

10

11

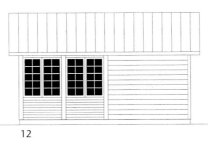

12

13

15　*Site plan*

16　*Bunkie interior looking north*

Photography: Celia Pearson

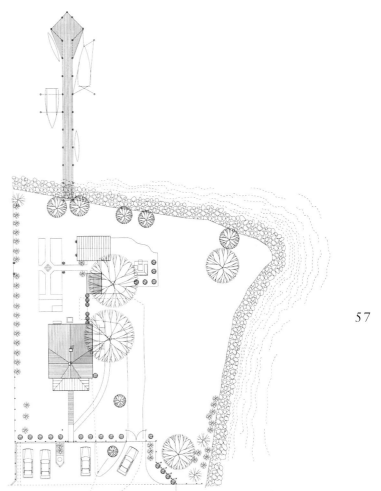

15

57

16

1

1 *View from Crab Creek*

2 *Approach view from front lawn*

Opposite *Front elevation from northwest corner*

House of Roggio

This house and project were inspired by the work of the great "gentlemen" architects, quietly practicing at the turn of the century through the 1930s. Many of the finest American country houses were created during this unique and prolific building period by such innovative architects as Harrie T. Lindeberg, John Russell Pope, and Frank J. Forster. Progressive in their skillful adaptation of historical types to the contemporary needs and desires of their clients, but not avant-garde, their work was often eclipsed by the incoming tide of the modern movement in America. It is only recently that these architects have been rediscovered and their work is now appreciated for its broad representation of American cultural values and refinement of domestic architectural taste in the traditional styles.

Situated on nine acres of beautiful rolling meadow overlooking Crab Creek near Annapolis, Maryland, the clients' desire was to create a new residence with an English

influence in the manner of the traditional, picturesque American country house. The clients also wished to evoke an aura of age and hand craftsmanship as a backdrop to their growing collection of antique English furnishings. The site was previously developed, and a severely neglected 1940s "Coca-colonial" was razed to make way for the new house. In addition to the many mature trees on the site, an existing tennis court, large free-form swimming pool, and boat house were retained, renovated, and incorporated into the overall site planning scheme.

Resolving the clients' contemporary functional requirements, living patterns, and ubiquitous desire for maximum openness to water views offered by the site, without corrupting the scale and character that define the English type, was a primary design challenge. Cost-effective techniques were devised to achieve a high level of hand detail in the woodwork. A study of furniture of the period provided inspiration for the

resolution of many architectural design problems. For example, the floor-to-ceiling windows of the great room, recessed behind the stone arches of the waterfront loggia, were inspired by an early, glazed, break-front china cabinet. The details of the entry porch columns were inspired by simple, decoratively chamfered table legs in a "cupid's bow" motif.

2

4

5

6

7

8

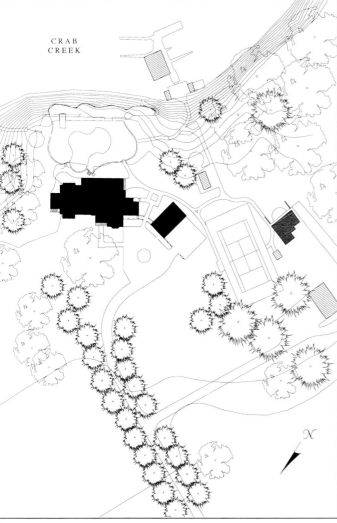

9

10

CRAB
CREEK

N

4 *View of covered walk and main house from garage drive*

5 *Roofscape view from guest bedroom*

6 *Southeast corner: breakfast room and loggia*

7 *Garage from breakfast loggia*

8 *View of loggia through stone arch*

9 *Site plan*

10 *Covered walk to mudroom entry from garage*

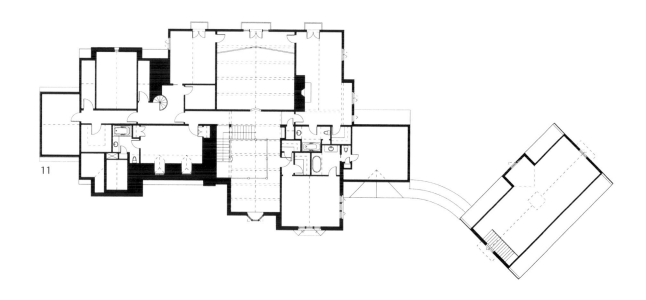

11

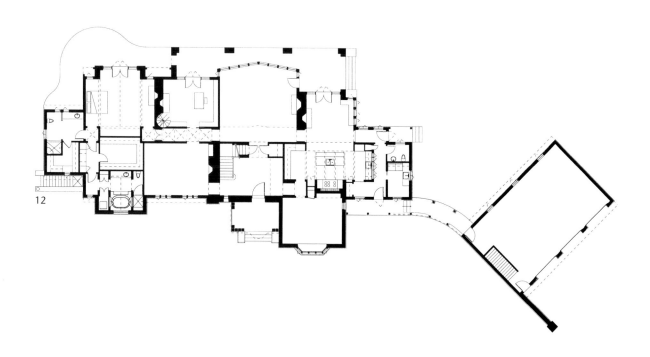

12

13

14

15

11 *Second floor plan*

12 *First floor plan*

13 *Detail of entry porch*

14 *Front entry*

15 *Stair hall*

16 *South elevation*

16

17

64

18

19

20

21

22

17   *Schematic waterfront elevation*

18   *Breakfast room*

19   *Schematic approach elevation*

20   *Living room*

21   *Dining room*

22   *View from upper level of stair hall*

23

24

23 Library

24 English guest bedroom

25 Kitchen

Photography: Celia Pearson

25

1 *Loggia*

2 *East elevation*

Opposite *View on approach from drive*

1

Roggio Cottage

As phase one of a larger residential compound, this project was designed to serve as temporary living quarters for the client while the main residence was being constructed. Adapted from a rather nondescript three-car garage structure existing on the property, this small cottage eventually became a guesthouse to the main residence.

Located on nine acres of beautiful rolling meadow overlooking Crab Creek near Annapolis, Maryland, the entire project was executed in the manner of American Tudor—inspired by the great picturesque mansions built in this country in the 1920s and early 30s by such innovative architects as Harrie T. Lindeberg, John Russell Pope, and Frank J. Forster. While the main house is a serious and authentic interpretation of early half-timber and stone domestic architecture, the guest cottage has been rendered as a more playful garden folly.

EAST ELEVATION

ROGGIO GUEST HOUSE

concept design

2

5

6

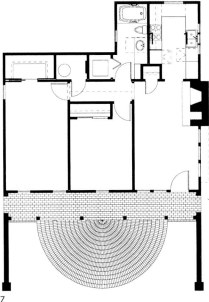

7

4 Waterside elevation

5 Detail of timber gable

6 Living room

7 Cottage floor plan

Photography: Celia Pearson

Kyle Residence

The community of Sherwood Forest near Annapolis, Maryland began in 1913 as a summer retreat for family rest and recreation. Developed on a 467-acre peninsula along the Severn River, the community was planned around preserved common areas, which include a community center, a general store, a post office, and a golf course. The original summer homes were sited in the surrounding woodlands and built close together in the manner of small Adirondack camp cottages with horizontal lapped siding often employing handcrafted locust pole ornaments and railings.

Today the community is undergoing a metamorphosis of sorts transitioning into a year-round community. The decision to take up full time residency typically results in the need for three or more times the square footage of the original summer cottages. This house addresses the challenges of inserting larger houses into the community while maintaining and reinforcing the original architectural spirit, character, and integrity of the community.

Sited on a high bluff with panoramic river views, the house was designed as a series of four individual "cottages," each carefully sized to evoke the scale and image of an original Sherwood Forest cottage. The plan was staggered to minimize the apparent mass and to create a pocket of outdoor privacy for the owners. The approach image of the house is closed and dominated by a playfully small-scaled semi-detached entry "cottage." This structure acts as an element of transition and imparts an overall impression of diminutive scale to the entire house. Upon entry, the scale shifts and the interior spaces begin to open up, revealing and relating to the larger, panoramic river views.

2

1 *Detail of entry pavilion*

2 *Site plan*

Opposite *Woodland view*

4

5

6

7

9

8

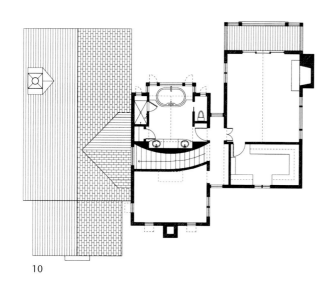

10

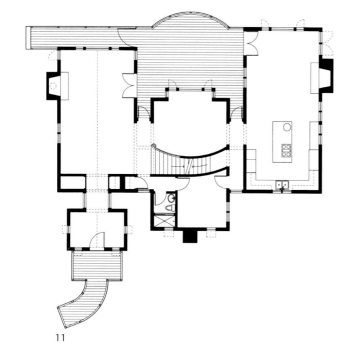

11

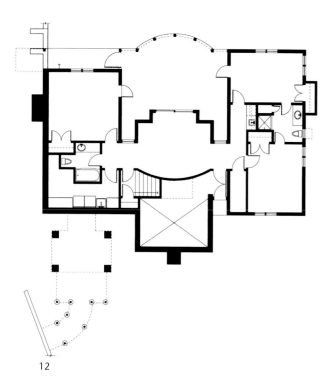

12

13

14

Photography: Celia Pearson

15

16

1

2

Corckran Residence

Sited on a compact lot at the toe of a long peninsula on the Severn River near Annapolis, Maryland, this project is located in a community that was modeled after the summer camps found along the northern and eastern United States at the turn of the century. Originally a summer retreat, the community is composed primarily of cottage-like houses with an odd but compatible scattering of gambrel roofed houses and other structures which present a slightly bolder presence than the more common cottages. This house was designed in the same spirit of summer architecture as inspired by the work of William R. Emerson.

Strict architectural design requirements including control of sight lines by all neighboring property owners largely impacted the design. It was determined that the employment of a similar gambrel roof design at this prominent location would provide an effective device to visually lower,

soften, and moderate the difficult massing problems of a full three-story house. A complex height, massing, and plan envelope was granted within which to arrange the client's spatial requirements. Light and views were of paramount importance and the plan was designed to segment and enhance what is essentially a single panoramic river view into multiple views unique to each space. Eccentricities of the allowed building envelope were exploited into many positive attributes of the house such as the 18-foot serpentine wall of bi-folding glass panels which allows the kitchen and breakfast room to be completely opened up.

1   *View from river*

2   *View from approach road*

Opposite   *Riverfront elevation*

4

80

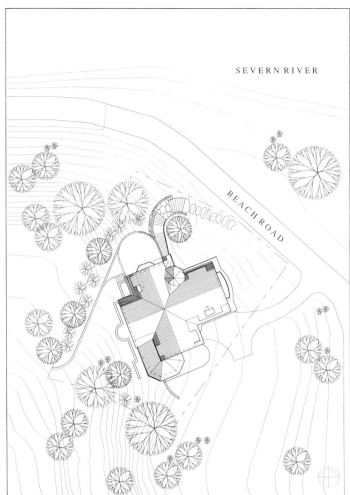

SEVERN RIVER

BEACH ROAD

5

4 *Dining deck*

5 *Site plan*

6 *Serpentine window-wall*

7 *View of stair and living room*

8 *Main stair*

9 *East elevation*

6

7

8

9

Photography: Celia Pearson

10

11

12

13

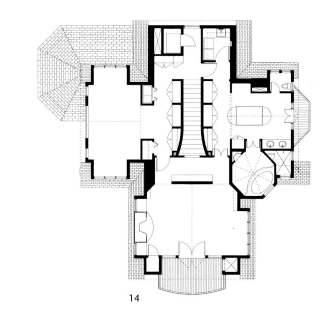

14

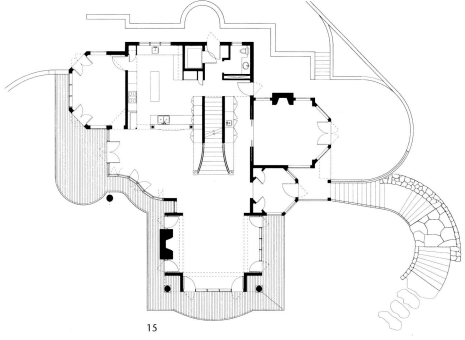

15

16

1

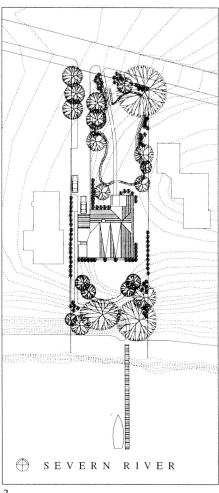

SEVERN RIVER

2

Brown-Nebel Residence

Sited on a gentle knoll overlooking Round Bay on the Severn River near Annapolis, Maryland, this project involved additions and the complete remodeling of a small, outmoded, 1930s Cape Cod Colonial house. Inspired by Edwin Lutyen's Tigbourne Court and Homewood, the triple-gable composition provides a pleasant architectural character and a human scale on approach. At the same time, the super-scaled opening of the center balcony establishes a strong presence for the house that relates to the greater riverscape.

The expanded and remodeled spaces within accommodate a new entry foyer, living room, kitchen, dining room, and large open family room on the first floor, and a master bedroom/bathroom suite and private balcony on the second floor. A covered loggia, created by recessing gently curved floor-to-ceiling windows under the gables, floods the principal spaces with soft natural light and panoramic water views.

3

5

6

7

8

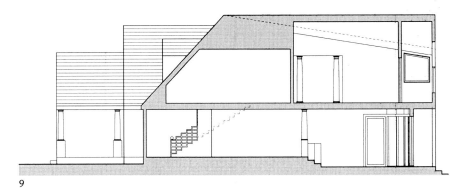

9

5   *View from screened balcony*

6   *Upper living room*

7   *View from loggia*

8   *Lower living room*

9   *Building section*

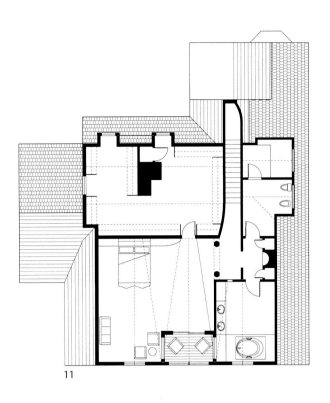

11

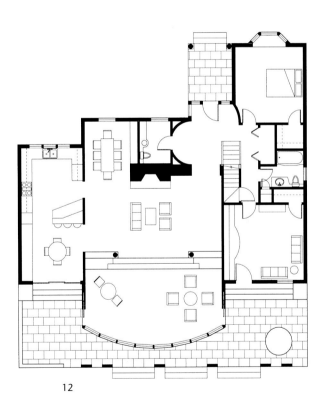

12

Opposite *Breakfast room and kitchen*

11 *Second floor plan*

12 *First floor plan*

Photography: *Celia Pearson*

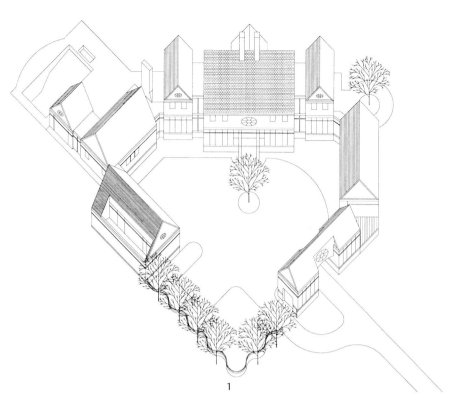

1

1 *Isometric view*

2 *Glass "hyphen" connecting*
kitchen to dining room

Opposite *View on approach from winding drive*

Love's End

The Chesapeake Bay Tidewater region is a veritable museum of many of the finest examples of 18th-century American Georgian domestic architecture. These houses are early symbols of an emerging American culture and gentility, and can be seen to possess a kind of architectural genetic code for the region. While contemporary in program and execution, this new house distills and reflects both the casual charm of a classic tidewater country manor and the graceful formality of the great 18th-century Georgian houses of Annapolis.

With a site that offered a 270-degree water view, it was determined to avoid a single large structure that otherwise seemed inevitable, given the rather extensive programmatic requirements for the house. The resulting design is a series of one-room-deep outbuildings, each housing a different function: kitchen, guest rooms, office, garage, and screened porch—all connected with glass "hyphens" and anchored by the classic five-part plan. From the auto court, only glimpses of the water beyond can be seen through the hyphens; the major water views have been carefully withheld and choreographed to slowly reveal themselves only upon entering and as one moves about throughout the house. The arrangement of functions around a central court affords every space unique water views, balanced natural illumination, and good cross-ventilation.

2

4

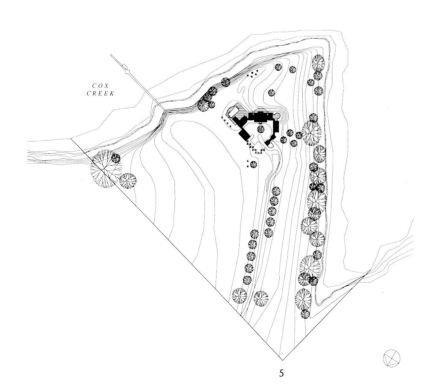

COX
CREEK

5

6

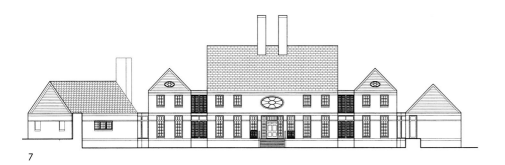

7

8

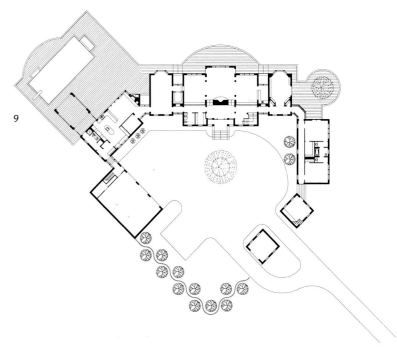

9

10

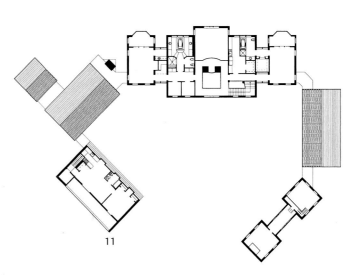

11

Photography: *Celia Pearson*

1

Asagao

A private residence, this house was created for an individual who acquired a deep love and appreciation for Japanese domestic architecture, while living in Japan for a number of years. The design of this house was inspired by 16th-century Japanese *Sukiya*, or "tea house" architecture. The architectural design attempts to express the ideals of *wabi*, which converted the tea ceremony into an occasion for withdrawal from material concerns and worship of purity and refinement. Planned on a traditional *tatami* grid (approximately 3 feet x 6 feet), the resulting design is a hybrid with influences from many historic, as well as contemporary examples of actual *Sukiya* houses in Japan.

While the house and appendages were constructed by employing typical western platform framing techniques, the surrounding *engawa*, or porch structure, was fabricated in a post-and-beam manner by craftsmen with experience in Japanese joinery.

The site is situated approximately 3 miles west of Easton, Maryland, on the Miles River in Talbot County. A unique aspect of the site is its position, which enjoys a long 4-mile southwesterly view down the river to Chesapeake Bay. The site itself was previously a flat characterless soybean field. All of the ponds and landscape were created as part of the project.

1   *Front elevation*

2   *Site plan*

Opposite   *House set on stone piers with floating porch*

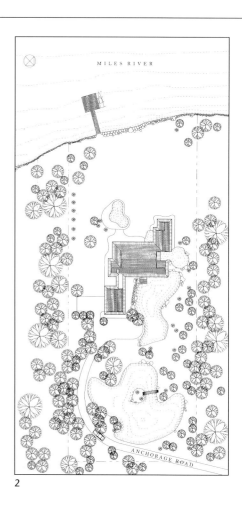

2

4

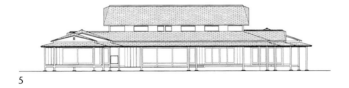

5

6

4   *View from living room*

5   *South elevation*

6   *East elevation*

7   *Sliding panels allow living room*
     to be open to outdoors

8   *View of house corner over pond*

9   *Second floor plan*

10 *First floor plan*

Photography: Taylor Lewis

7

8

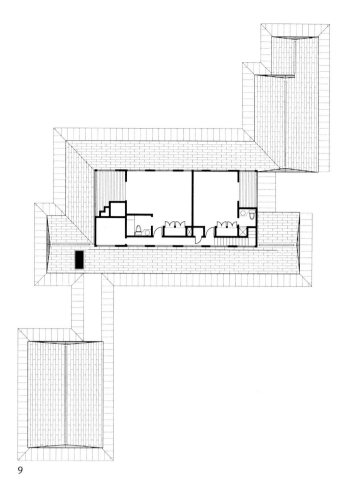

9

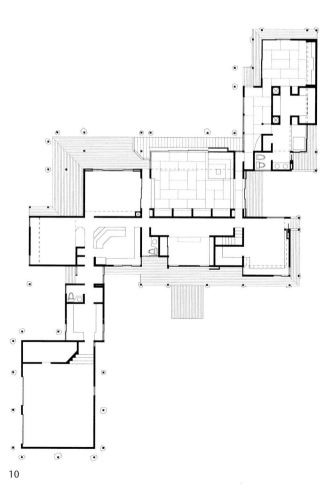

10

 1

2

Beverly Plantation (under construction)

Believing that it is really "hip to be square," this new house eschews the current faddism of bizarre form-making and chooses instead to add a link to the chain of tradition by reflecting the 300-year-old Anglo-architectural legacy of its regional location. A direct descendent of the brick architecture of the Colonial period in Maryland, the design of this modern Maryland manor is the result of a synthesis of diverse ancestral architectural characteristics. Functionally, the house is thoroughly contemporary while achieving an architectural dignity and repose that are otherwise gained only through the passage of time.

In the 18th century, proximity to waterways was generally viewed as a necessary means of commerce and transportation but was also considered to be a source of disease. Therefore most plantation houses were sited away from the water's edge focusing instead on formal gardens. Of course, today the

water view is paramount, and the demand for over-scaled areas of glass presents a unique design challenge to the integrity of the timeless architecture and human scale of the traditional house.

The center block and main living room of this new house was inspired by a rare and unique 18th-century building type—the Orangerie. Essentially a conservatory, these functional but decorative garden structures were used by the wealthy for wintering-over fragile plants, especially citrus trees, which were valued for their medicinal qualities. In studying this building type, it was determined that the uniquely large area of glass was gracefully adaptable to the natural daylight and water-view desires of contemporary lifestyles. Responding to specific circumstances and requirements of the land, the plan of the house is both formal and casual providing a pleasant variety of circulation axes, spaces, and

orientations. Currently under construction, this new-old house promises to inspire new pathways to integrating meaningful tradition into the domestic architecture of the present and the future.

1   *Main entry*

2   *View from pier*

Opposite   *View from north lawn*

4

River Room

5

6

7

8

101

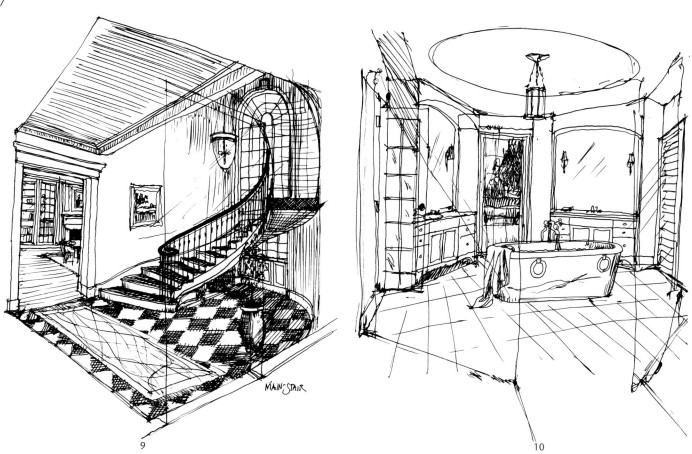

MAIN STAIR

9

10

102   *Photography:* Celia Pearson

1

Mackowiak Residence

Perched on the edge of a steep and deep ravine, this Adirondack-styled cottage captures breathtaking panoramic water views while fitting into and reinforcing the context of a community of small cottages. Split in two by an interior cascading staircase which dramatically frames a two-story, surprise view across the ravine upon entering, the floor plan and interior were designed to evoke fond memories of a family cottage that the owners grew up in.

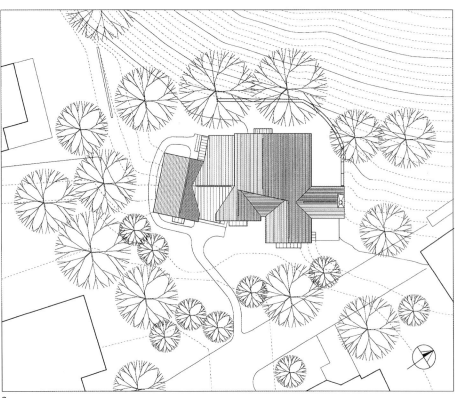

2

3

4

5

6

1

Collins Residence

Sited on a bluff overlooking the Chesapeake Bay in Maryland, this project involved new additions and the remodeling of outmoded spaces within a 1930s house. The original house had been poorly added to and remodeled over the years resulting in an undesirable massing and characterless architectural expression.

Initially, the client's program called for the conversion of an existing attached garage into a new family room and the addition of a new detached two-car garage to replace the old one. The new garage was designed to

achieve architectural symmetry and balance with an existing wing on the south end of the house. An open breezeway and colonnade were employed to organize the overall approach elevation. As the project progressed, the client recognized the positive transformation made by the placement of the garage. The program grew to include a complete remodeling of the master bedroom and bathroom suite, custom-designed light fixtures, and other decorative architectural elements lending overall balance and architectural cohesiveness to the house.

1 *View on approach*
2 *East elevation*
Opposite *Garage from garden entry*

2

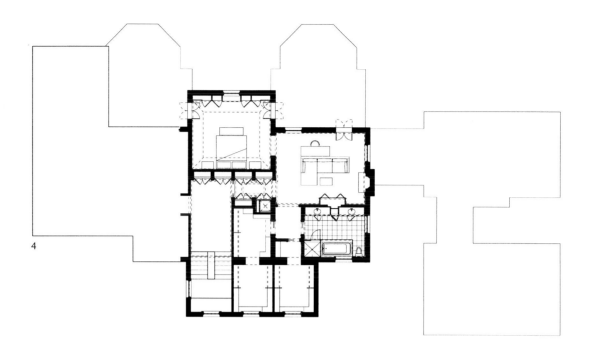

4

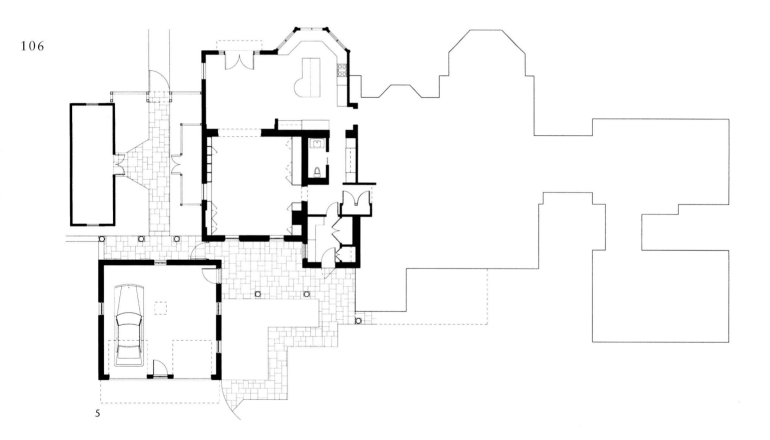

5

6

7

8

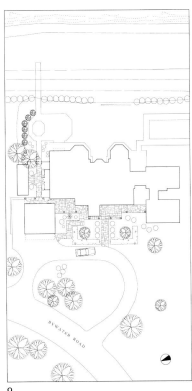

9

4 Second floor plan

5 First floor plan

6 West elevation

7 Southwest view of
garage addition

8 Dining room
sunscreen canopy

9 Site plan

Photography: *Celia Pearson*

Sarasota Residence

Located in the Sanderling Beach Club, on Siesta Key, near Sarasota, Florida, this project involved renovation and remodeling of an existing circa 1960s beach house. The house was built by an heir to a major national lumber supply house and is full of exotic woodwork. Designed in a quasi-Japanese motif, the house sits about 70 feet from the shoreline of the Gulf of Mexico to the west, and about 50 feet to the edge of a beautiful still-water lagoon to the east. Elevated about 3 feet above the sand on wood pilings, during storm tides the Gulf waters will actually roll up and under the house to the lagoon beyond.

The architects were asked to suggest economical ideas to simplify the architecture of the house in a way that is more evocative of the *Sukiya* or "tea house" style of Japanese architecture and to correct some rather eccentric design features such as the unsafe telephone pole steps leading to the main entry.

Generally, the architects responded by removing decorative rafter tails (more evocative of Chinese architecture); adding deeper, open-ribbed, *engawa* overhangs to filter the sunlight and lower the horizon, and adding a traditional Japanese wooden garden bridge as a means of entry to the elevated first floor. The new entry bridge will be landscaped with a metaphorical stone river leading to the lagoon.

1   *Sketch of new entry bridge*
2   *Floor plan*

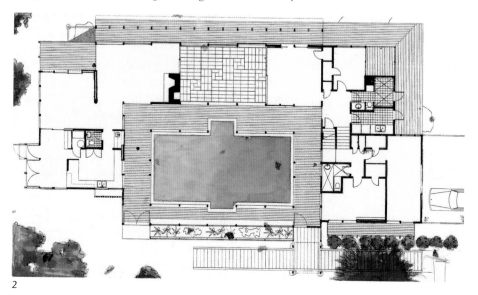

2

1

1 *Front elevation*
2 *East elevation*
3 *Second floor*
4 *First floor*
Photography: *Celia Pearson*

2

Johnson Residence

Located on an urban wooded corner lot in Annapolis, Maryland, this modest house for a young family of four was sited and composed to maximize privacy in the rear yard from the two sides exposed to the street. Designed as a series of 16-foot-wide gabled pavilions, each is connected by a glass "hyphen" which houses the stair and bathroom functions while admitting natural daylight to the interior in a unique way. Strong axial circulation paths all terminate with framed views giving the interior an unexpected sense of spaciousness.

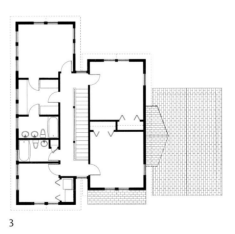

3

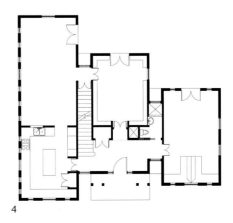

4

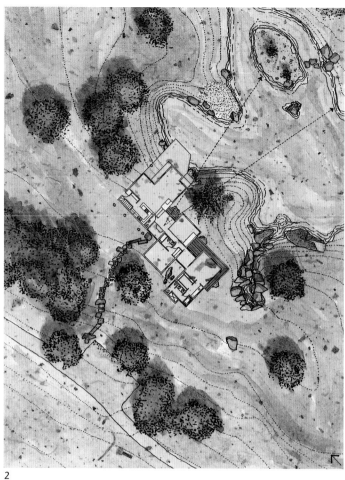

Sakura

Sakura, meaning "cherry tree," was designed as a private weekend retreat for an individual with a deep appreciation of Zen philosophy, the tea ceremony, and its influence on Japanese domestic architecture. The design of this house was inspired by 16th-century Japanese *Sukiya*, or "tea house," architecture and attempts to express the ideals of *wabi*—a set of ideals which converted the tea ceremony into an occasion for withdrawal from material concerns and worship of simplicity, purity, and refinement.

The building site consists of five secluded, wooded acres of land, at the base of a foothill of the Taconic Range near Rhinebeck, New York in Duchess County. Over the past five years, the owners have "camped" on the site while designing and building an extensive strolling and contemplation garden, which incorporates a natural waterfall and two streams feeding into a scenic koi pond with an island. The garden was designed to enhance all of the site's natural assets. Designed simply as three connected pavilions stepped diagonally, the plan arrangement symbolizes the pattern of geese in flight. The house is situated at the edge of the pond with easterly views across the water to the mountains beyond. A "moon viewing" platform overhanging the water will provide meditative views of the moon and its reflection as it rises over the mountains.

1 *Moonlight view across pond*

2 *Site plan*

Savage Residence

Located on the boundary of the
Annapolis Historic District, this project
involved a family room and swimming pool
addition to the rear yard of a small 1930s
Cape Cod Colonial house. The new addition
accommodates a spacious family room
opening directly onto the pool terrace
through french doors. Generous floor-to-
ceiling windows bring light and garden
views into the new space.

1   *View from pool*
2   *Living room*
Photography: *Wayne L. Good*

1

Fulton Residence

Sited on a bluff overlooking Otter Pond on Gibson Island, this new 2500-square-foot residence was designed for a retired couple. Evocative of traditional Maryland manor houses, the first floor accommodates all living functions for the owners while the walk-out below-grade level provides water-view guest rooms for family and friends, with a private deck and access to the pier and lake.

1 *Sketch of front elevation on approach*

2 *Site plan*

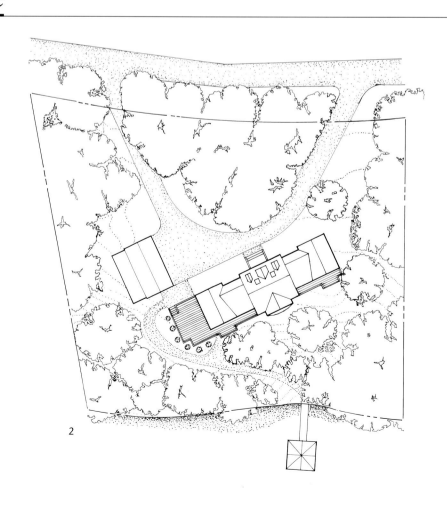

2

113

Gallagher Residence

This turn-of-the-century Georgian Revival house, located in the Annapolis Historic District, was extensively restored to accommodate a young family of six. Also included in the project was the addition of a swimming pool and contemporary but compatible two-car garage with a studio above. All new work was carefully designed for sympathetic integration within the historic context and to meet the requirements of the Secretary of the Interior's Standards for Historic Rehabilitation.

1 *Front elevation from street*
Photography: *Celia Pearson*

1

114

O'Hare Residence

Overlooking Spa Creek within the Annapolis Historic District, this project involved additions and remodeling to a small, outmoded, 1920s brick Dutch Colonial house. The new 2000-square-foot addition accommodates an entry foyer and large open family room on the first floor with a master bedroom/bathroom suite and private balcony on the second floor. Previously, the front door opened directly into a dark, too-tight hallway and staircase leading directly into the kitchen. The new entry re-orients the internal circulation, which provides an elegant arrival space, leading directly into the new all-glass family room with panoramic views of the historic harbor and its picturesque setting of visiting boats at anchor.

2

3

4

5

6

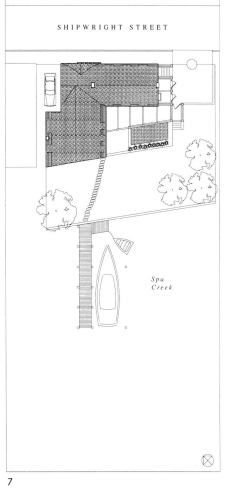

Spa Creek

7

1   *View from Spa Creek*

2   *Northeast elevation*

3   *Southwest elevation*

4   *Pool and new arbor*

5   *Main entry*

6   *Waterfront elevation from lawn*

7   *Site plan*

Photography: *Wayne L. Good*

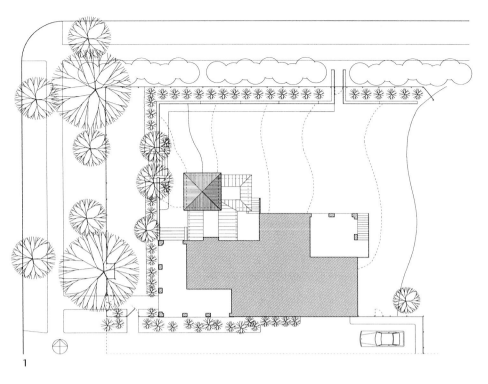

Kaye-McKean Residence

This circa 1920s Mediterranean-style stucco house, located in the Historic District of Cleveland Park in Washington, D.C. was extensively remodeled to accommodate the needs of a growing young family. Initially the interior and exterior of the existing house were remodeled including a new kitchen, bathrooms, and outdoor dining loggia. Five years later, the clients returned with the request for the addition of a new library and children's bedrooms and bathrooms. These functions were architecturally accommodated in a new glass room and stucco tower added to the corner of the house. Located on a prominent corner lot, the local preservation commission honored the project with an award for its superb example of compatible additions to an historic house.

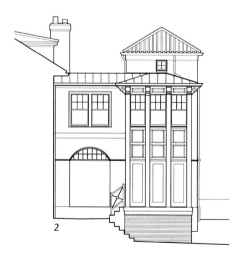

1   *Site plan*

2   *East elevation*

Opposite   *View of new addition*

Photography: *Celia Pearson*

Brunner-Russell Residence

Designed for two art consultants and their young growing family, this project involved extensive remodeling of a small existing 1920s Dutch Colonial house on a very tight lot near Washington, D.C. The client's request for a new studio space could only be accommodated by going up. By lifting the back of the gambrel roof and creating a continuous band of 12-inch by 12-inch clerestory windows on all four elevations, a wonderfully light and airy studio space was created from an otherwise uninhabitable attic space.

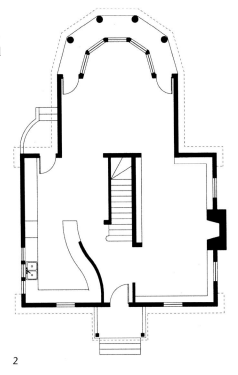

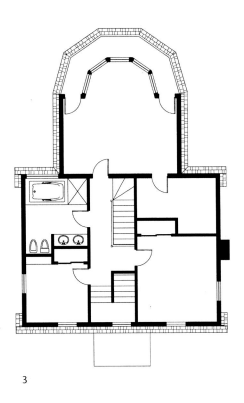

2

3

4

5

1 *Living room*

2 *First floor plan*

3 *Second floor plan*

4 *Artist's loft*

5 *Library*

1

2

3

Michaelson Residence

Overlooking Spa Creek in the Annapolis Historic District, this waterfront project involved complete restoration and additions to a circa 1915 Dutch Colonial house. The architecture of the existing gambrel roof house was precisely maintained in its historic detail while the new additions, nearly doubling the house, were designed in a distinctly contemporary but architecturally compatible form. Formal entry was maintained through the original center hall of the old house. This allows an elegant and surprising unfolding of views as one emerges from the traditional spaces of the old house into the openness of the new spaces, offering the contrast of dramatic panoramic water views and abundant natural daylight.

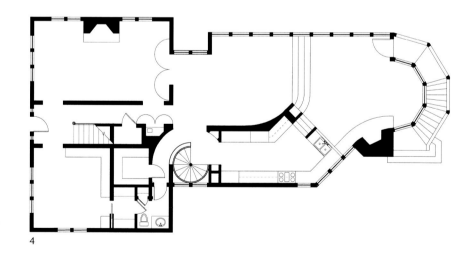
4

1 *North elevation*
2 *South elevation*
3 *View from Spa Creek*
4 *Floor plan*
Photography: *Celia Pearson*

1 *Poolside elevation*

2 *Street elevation*

Georgetown Residence (construction 2004)

Located on a corner site in the heart of Georgetown in Washington D.C., this circa 19th-century three-story brick Italianate townhouse required an extensive combination of interior and exterior restoration, renovation, and remodeling. Currently underway, additions of a new historically compatible brick poolhouse, garage, garden walls, and landscaping will bring this handsome residence functionally into the 21st century.

Saint Mary's Office

Asked by one of our residential clients to design a 40,000-square-foot professional office building on a steeply sloping wooded site near historic Saint Mary's City, we responded with a design which reinterprets characteristics of the late English medieval architecture first brought to the area by early British colonists. Gently curving along the edge of a natural bank on the site, the building is entered on two levels.

3

2

1 *Conceptual sketch*

2 *Arch detail*

3 *Bird's eye view of computer model*

"The architect is an artist or he is nothing.
It is true that he faces his problems with a
whole armoury of resources. He has delved
into the secrets of construction, which makes
him akin to the engineer. He has knowledge
of materials which stamps him as own brother
to the mason and carpenter. He has the
instinct for site, for ground forms, which
allies him to the landscape gardener. But
none of these things avail him if he is without
the sensitiveness and creative urge of the
artist. He may study endlessly and may
have passed through arduous scholastic
examinations but let him lack inspiration,
let him have no dreams, and he will function
only in terms of the commonplace."

— Royal Cortissoz

Excerpted from his 1940 introduction to
Domestic Architecture by H.T. Lindberg

Project details

Thompson Residence (2002)

Project Team: Wayne L. Good, David Mallon, Laura Kaupp, Elizabeth Schuncke

Owners: Ken and Helen Thompson

Contractor: Winchester Construction Company, Inc.

Landscape Architecture: Graham Landscape Architecture

Interior Design: The Grande Finale, Julia Beatty

Structural Engineer: John F. Rickert, P.E., Inc.

Awards and Publications:

2003 AIA Chesapeake Bay Honor Award for Excellence in Architectural Design

2003, *Another 100 of the World's Best Houses,* The Images Publishing Group

Rendering: Laura Kaupp

Island House (2002)

Project Team: Wayne L. Good, Laura Kaupp

Owners: Jo Ricks and Jeff Clark

Contractor: A&A Painting and Restoration, Mike Adams

Landscape Architecture: by Owner

Interior Design: by Architect

Structural Engineer: John F. Rickert, P.E., Inc.

Awards:

2003 AIA Baltimore/*Baltimore Magazine* Award for Distinctive Residential Architecture

2002 AIA Maryland Society Citation for Excellence in Architectural Design

2002 AIA Chesapeake Bay Honor Award for Excellence in Architectural Design

Rendering: Laura Kaupp

Dillow Hall (2001)

Project Team: Wayne L. Good, Brian Bassindale, David Mallon

Owners: Mark and Joanne Dillow

Contractor: by Owner

Landscape Architecture: Stratton Semmes Landscape Architecture; Graham Landscape Architecture

Interior Design: Mona Hajj Interior Design

Structural Engineer: John F. Rickert, P.E., Inc.

Awards and Publications:

2001 AIA Maryland Society Commendation Award for Architectural Excellence

2001 AIA Baltimore/*Baltimore Magazine* Award for Distinctive Residential Architecture

2001 AIA Chesapeake Bay Honor Award for Excellence in Architectural Design

November/December 2001, *Custom Home,* "Design Directions: Sum of Parts"

October 2001, *Baltimore Magazine,* "Inside Stories"

Rendering: Wayne L. Good

Timberlane Farm (2000)

Project Team: Wayne L. Good, Brian Bassindale, David Mallon

Contractor: Winchester Construction Company, Inc.

Landscape Architecture: Graham Landscape Architecture

Interior Design: Mona Hajj Interior Design

Structural Engineer: John F. Rickert, P.E., Inc.

Awards and Publications:

2000 AIA Maryland Society Merit Award for Excellence in Architectural Design

2000 AIA Baltimore/*Baltimore Magazine* Award for Distinctive Residential Architecture

2000 AIA Chesapeake Bay Merit Award for Excellence in Architectural Design

Winter 2002, *Washington Maryland Virginia Home and Design,* "Casual Elegance"

2002, *A Decade of Art & Architecture,* The Institute of Classical Architecture

October 2000, *Baltimore Magazine,* "Tailored to Fit"

September/October 2000, *Chesapeake Life,* "Masters' Plans"

Rendering: Wayne L. Good (12); Laura Kaupp (3, 7, 8)

Moore Residence (1999)

Project Team: Wayne L. Good, David Mallon

Owners: Don and Suzy Moore

Contractor: Smith & Orwig Builders

Landscape Architecture: Stratton Semmes Landscape Architecture

Interior Design: by Owner

Structural Engineer: John F. Rickert, P.E., Inc.

Awards and Publications:

2000 AIA Maryland Society Citation for Excellence in Architectural Design

2001 AIA Baltimore/*Baltimore Magazine* Award for Distinctive Residential Architecture

1999 AIA Chesapeake Bay Citation for Excellence in Architectural Design

October 2001, *Baltimore Magazine,* "Dueling Architects"

Rendering: David Mallon

Tatum Residence (1999)

Project Team: Wayne L. Good, Brian Bassindale, David Mallon

Owners: Liston and Corinne Tatum

Contractor: Freeman Builders, Howard Freeman

Landscape Architecture: Stratton Semmes Landscape Architecture

Interior Design: by Owner

Structural Engineer: John F. Rickert, P.E., Inc.

Awards and Publications:

2001 *Residential Architect* Design Awards Merit Award

1999 AIA Maryland Society Citation for
Excellence in Architectural Design
1999 AIA Baltimore/*Baltimore Magazine* Award
for Distinctive Residential Architecture
1999 AIA Chesapeake Bay Honor Award for
Excellence in Architectural Design
2003, *Another 100 of the World's Best Houses*,
The Images Publishing Group
October 2001, *Chesapeake Life*,
"Cabin Contemporary"
May 2001, *Residential Architect*, "2001 Design
Awards"
October 1999, *Baltimore Magazine*, "A Simple Plan"
Rendering: Laura Kaupp

Mosquito Bight (1999)

Project Team: Wayne L. Good
Owners: Wayne and Leslie Good
Contractor: by Owner
Landscape Architecture: by Owner
Interior Design: by Owner
Structural Engineer: John F. Rickert, P.E., Inc.
Publications:
August 2001, *Style*, "American Beauty"
July 13, 2000, *The Washington Post*, "A Fine Catch"

House of Roggio (1998)

Project Team: Wayne L. Good, Brian Bassindale,
David Mallon
Owners: Bob and Mary Roggio
Contractor: Smith and Orwig Builders, Inc.
Landscape Architecture: Stratton Semmes
Landscape Architecture
Interior Design: by Owner
Structural Engineer: John F. Rickert, P.E., Inc.
Awards and Publications:
1998 AIA Chesapeake Bay Award of Merit for
Excellence in Architectural Design
1998 AIA Maryland Society Honor Award for
Excellence in Architectural Design
August 30, 2003, *The Capital*, "Stonewater offers
luxury retreat"
September 2000, *Custom Home*, "Tudor Coup"
2002, *A Decade of Art & Architecture*, The Institute
of Classical Architecture
Rendering: Wayne L. Good

Roggio Cottage (1996)

Project Team: Wayne L. Good, Brian Bassindale,
David Mallon
Owners: Bob and Mary Roggio
Contractor: Smith and Orwig Builders, Inc.
Landscape Architecture: Stratton Semmes
Landscape Architecture
Interior Design: by Owner

Structural Engineer: John F. Rickert, P.E., Inc.
Awards and Publications:
1998 AIA Baltimore/*Baltimore Magazine* Award
for Distinctive Residential Architecture
1996 AIA Maryland Society Award of Merit for
Excellence in Architectural Design
October 1998, *Baltimore Magazine*, "Designs of
the Times"
May 30, 1998, *The Capital*,
"A Magical Transformation"
January 1998, *Residential Architect*,
"Home Sweet Garage"
Summer 1997, *Freehand*, "1996 AIA Maryland
Design Awards"
December 15, 1996, *The Sunday Capital*,
"Building on a Good Name"
Rendering: Wayne L. Good

Kyle Residence (1995)

Project Team: Wayne L. Good, Brian Bassindale
Owners: Tom and Gage Kyle
Contractor: Winchester Construction
Company, Inc.
Landscape Architecture: Andy Hobson
Interior Design: by Owner
Structural Engineer: John F. Rickert, P.E., Inc.
Awards and Publications:
1998 AIA Baltimore/*Baltimore Magazine* Award
for Distinctive Residential Architecture
1996 AIA Chesapeake Bay Merit Award for
Excellence in Architectural Design
January/February 1999, *Residential Architect*,
"Local Color"
October 1998, *Baltimore Magazine*,
"Designs of the Times"

Corckran Residence (1990)

Project Team: Wayne L. Good, Brian Bassindale
Owners: Jim and Jenny Corckran
Contractor: Winchester Construction
Company, Inc.
Landscape Architecture: Stratton Semmes
Landscape Architecture
Interior Design: Brandy DeVries
Structural Engineer: John F. Rickert, P.E., Inc.
Awards:
1996 AIA Chesapeake Bay Citation for Excellence
in Architectural Design

Brown-Nebel Residence (1989)

Project Team: Wayne L. Good, Brian Bassindale,
Laura Kaupp
Owners: John Brown and Janet Nebel
Contractor: Phase I Choice Builders, Mark
Wagner; Phase II Winchester Construction
Company, Inc.

Landscape Architecture: Stratton Semmes
Landscape Architecture
Interior Design: by Owner
Structural Engineer: John F. Rickert, P.E., Inc.
Awards and Publications:
1993 AIA Baltimore/*Baltimore Magazine* Award
for Distinctive Residential Architecture
1992 AIA Chesapeake Bay Honor Award for
Excellence in Architectural Design
April 1994, *Mid Atlantic Country Magazine*,
"Return of the Porch"
October 1993, *Baltimore Magazine*,
"Perfectly at Home"
June 1993, *Baltimore Magazine*, "A River Runs By It"
April 1993, *Annapolis Magazine*, "Taking Advantage
of a View"

Love's End (1989)

Project Team: Wayne L. Good, Brian Bassindale,
Janet Shenk
Owners: Cornelius and Carole Love
Contractor: Winchester Construction
Company, Inc.
Landscape Architecture: Andy Hobson,
Wayne L. Good
Interior Design: by Owner
Structural Engineer: John F. Rickert, P.E., Inc.
Awards and Publications:
1996 AIA Maryland Society Citation for
Excellence in Architectural Design
1995 *Builder Magazine* Top Seven Custom
Houses of 1995
1993 AIA Chesapeake Bay Merit Award for
Excellence in Architectural Design
November/December 2000, *Custom Home*,
"Estate Planning"
Summer 1997, *Freehand*, "1996 AIA Maryland
Design Awards"
December 15, 1996, *The Sunday Capital*,
"Building on a Good Name"
June 1995, *Builder Magazine*, "By the Bay"
Winter 1994/1995, *Freehand*, "1993 Awards:
AIA/CBC"
April 1994, *Glen-Gery Brickwork Design Magazine*,
"Love's End, Stevensville, MD"
February 1994, *Annapolis Magazine*,
"Winning Designs"
July 1992, *Annapolitan*, "State of 'Their Art'"

Asagao (1987)

Project Team: Wayne L. Good, Brian Bassindale,
Tim Donohue
Owners: John and Jenny Hyatt
Contractor: Winchester Construction
Company, Inc.
Landscape Architecture: Andy Hobson,
John Gutting

Interior Design: by Owner
Structural Engineer: John F. Rickert, P.E., Inc.
Awards and Publications:
1990 AIA Chesapeake Bay Honor Award for
    Excellence in Architectural Design
March 1998, *Residential Architect,*
    "Disappearing Doors"
May 9, 1994, *The Star-Democrat,* "Maryland
    House and Garden Pilgrimage"
1993, *Chesapeake: The Eastern Shore: Gardens
    Houses,* Simon and Schuster
November 24, 1991, *Baltimore Sun,*
    "An Eastern Vision"
May 10, 1991, *The Star Democrat,* "Asagao—
    A Touch of Japan on the Miles River"
September 1990, *Annapolitan,* "Build with Style"

Beverly Plantation (2004)
Project Team: Wayne L. Good, Brian Bassindale,
    David Mallon, Laura Kaupp
Owners: Jim and Joyce Kerridge
Contractor: Smith and Orwig Builders, Inc.
Landscape Architecture: Graham Landscape
    Architecture
Interior Design: by Owner
Structural Engineer: John F. Rickert, P.E., Inc.
Rendering: David Mallon

Mackowiak Residence (2000)
Project Team: Wayne L. Good, David Mallon
Owners: Dr and Mrs Philip Mackowiak
Contractor: Winchester Construction
    Company, Inc.
Interior Design: by Owner
Structural Engineer: John F. Rickert, P.E., Inc.

Collins Residence (2000)
Project Team: Wayne L. Good, Brian Bassindale,
    Tim Donohue
Owners: George and Maureen Collins
Contractor: Winchester Construction
    Company, Inc.
Interior Design: Lorraine Letendre
Structural Engineer: John F. Rickert, P.E., Inc.

Sarasota Residence (2001)
Project Team: Wayne L. Good, David Mallon
Owners: Bob and Mary Roggio
Contractor: MacInnes Construction,
    Wayne MacInnes
Interior Design: by Owner
Structural Engineer: John F. Rickert, P.E., Inc.
Awards:
1998 AIA Chesapeake Bay Intern Citation Award
    for Excellence in Architectural Design
Rendering: David Mallon

Johnson Residence (1997)
Project Team: Wayne L. Good, David Mallon
Owners: Steve and Martha Johnson
Contractor: Charlie Madison
Interior Design: by Owner
Structural Engineer: John F. Rickert, P.E., Inc.

Sakura (unbuilt)
Project Team: Wayne L. Good
Owner: Anthony Roland
Contractor: unbuilt
Awards:
1993 AIA Chesapeake Bay Merit Award for
    Excellence in Architectural Design
Winter 1994/1995, *Freehand,* "1993 Awards:
    AIA/CBC"
Rendering: Wayne L. Good

Savage Residence (1993)
Project Team: Wayne L. Good, Janet Shenk
Owners: Donald and Judith Savage
Contractor: F.R. Hawkins and Sons
Structural Engineer: John F. Rickert, P.E., Inc.

Fulton Residence (1989)
Project Team: Wayne L. Good, Brian Bassindale,
    Christine Dayton
Owners: Mr and Mrs Fulton
Contractor: Choice Builders, Mark Wagner
Interior Design: by Owner
Structural Engineer: John F. Rickert, P.E., Inc.
Rendering: Wayne L. Good

O'Hare Residence (1987)
Project Team: Wayne L. Good, Janet Shenk
Owners: Mr and Mrs O'Hare
Contractor: Richard Somer
Landscape Architecture: by Owner
Interior Design: by Owner
Structural Engineer: John F. Rickert, P.E., Inc.
Publications:
October 1991, *Annapolitan,* "The Right Mix"
Rendering: Wayne L. Good

Gallagher Residence (1992)
Project Team: Wayne L. Good, Brian Bassindale,
    Janet Shenk, Elizabeth Schuncke
Owners: Jack and Cathy Gallagher
Contractor: Winchester Construction
    Company, Inc.
Interior Design: by Owner
Structural Engineer: John F. Rickert, P.E., Inc.

Kaye-McKean Residence (1991)
Project Team: Wayne L. Good, Brian Bassindale,
    Tim Donohue, David Mallon
Owners: Kathleen Kaye and David McKean
Contractor: Artworks, Charlie Sleichter
Interior Design: by Owner
Structural Engineer: John F. Rickert, P.E., Inc.
Awards:
1993 Cleveland Park Historical Society
    Preservation Achievement Award for
    Excellence in Architectural Design

Brunner-Russell Residence (1987)
Project Team: Wayne L. Good
Owners: Don Russell and Helen Brunner
Contractor: Artworks, Charlie Sleichter
Landscape Architecture: Gay Crowther
Interior Design: by Owner
Structural Engineer: John F. Rickert, P.E., Inc.
Awards and Publications:
1990 AIA Chesapeake Bay Award for Excellence
    in Architectural Design
May 19, 1994, *The New York Times,* "From Crawl
    Space to Spacious Aerie"
September 30, 1990, *The Washington Post
    Magazine,* "A Clean Slate"

Michaelson Residence (1986)
Project Team: Wayne L. Good
Owners: Ben and Fran Michaelson
Contractor: Horizon Builders, George Fritz,
    Joe Bohm
Interior Design: by Owner
Structural Engineer: John F. Rickert, P.E., Inc.

Georgetown Residence (unbuilt)
Project Team: Wayne L. Good, Elizabeth Schuncke
Owners: David Goodhand
Contractor: Winchester Construction
    Company, Inc.
Interior Design: Barbara Leland Interior Design
Structural Engineer: John F. Rickert, P.E., Inc.

Saint Mary's Office (unbuilt)
Project Team: Wayne L. Good
Owner: Mark Dillow
Contractor: unbuilt
Rendering: Wayne L. Good

Good Architecture

Annapolis, Maryland

Established in 1986, Good Architecture is primarily engaged in the design of the private American house. Directed by Wayne L. Good, FAIA, the firm's work is guided by a profound belief in the dynamic and enduring qualities of traditional and classically inspired domestic architecture as a basis for contemporary design. Each project contributes to the firm's quest to understand the unique characteristics that distinguish the American house from all others. Often asked to build on sites with historic significance, the firm's architecture is characterized by a strong connection to place and a distinct dialogue with history. Wayne's houses are widely recognized for the skill with which he composes each client's unique vision into an exquisite architectural portrait of their personal dreams, memories, personality, and spirit of place. Although there is a common qualitative thread that runs through the firm's work, it is the obvious lack of a pronounced 'signature style' in the outward appearance of each project which reflects most clearly the individuality of each client and the broad diversity of American culture.

Wayne's approach to architecture is based on the idea that it is better to be good than to be original. Although a passionate observer of the contemporary architectural scene, he believes strongly that the 'cult of novelty' is pervasive within the profession and ultimately is the 'mother of mediocrity'. Through a process of reflective interpretation of familiar forms, context, and local culture as guided by the client's brief, the firm's architecture is informed with an enduring quality of domestic repose. His work demonstrates that architectural excellence can be achieved with less iconoclastic ideals than those aspired to by the trend followers. As a result, the firm's work has been honored with over forty local, regional, and national design awards, and has been widely published in regional and national media.

128